THE
SHOWER GENIUS

HOW SELF-CARE,
CREATIVITY AND SANITY
WILL CHANGE YOUR LIFE...
PERSONALLY & PROFESSIONALLY!

DEANA BROWN MITCHELL
GENIUS & SANITY

Year of the Book
135 Glen Ave.
Glen Rock, PA 17327

ISBN: 978-1-64649-289-3 (print)
ISBN: 978-1-64649-290-9 (ebook)

For my husband, Michael,
for his unending love and support
despite us being apart for work so many years.

CONTENTS

1   Welcome & Introduction 1

PHASE ONE: Acknowledge & Assess 9

2   Get Fed Up! 11

3   What Is My Sanity Level? 17

4   The Value of Ranting 23

5   Dream Away 31

PHASE TWO: Be Your Own Best Advocate & Take Action.... 39

6   Become M.I.A. 41

7   I Refuse 47

8   Be Intentional 55

9   Creativity 61

PHASE THREE: Growth & Freedom.. 67

10   Planning & Delegation 69

11   Implement 77

12   Growth & Results 83

13   Rinse & Repeat 89

14   My Hope For You 93

1 WELCOME & INTRODUCTION

I know what you must be thinking... what the heck is a shower genius? There are tons of books, articles, and tools out there that talk about how to beat stress and overwhelm while becoming more productive. You see titles like "*5 Ways to Increase Productivity*," "*8 Ways to Reduce Stress*," and "*4 Ways to Deal with Overwhelm*." But have you ever used the advice from one of those to create long-term success?

If you are like me, you try it once and say, "*I am going to do this every day*," but three days later you do not even remember what it was or why you committed to doing it.

Do you want a tip or trick for the moment, or do you want lasting change?

I mean the kind of change that will transform all parts of your personal and professional life. You cannot have one without the other. You can't have a perfect business life while your personal life is falling apart, or vice versa. One supports the other. They balance each other—but not the "work-life balance" that you hear people throw around all the time. There is no quick fix and likely you will be working on one or the other, but not both in sync.

> *Do you want a tip or trick for the moment, or do you want lasting change?*

You see, when we are at our desk, in meetings with clients, or driving our kids to school, our mind is focused on multiple things and cluttered. Over long periods of time, this creates overwhelm, stress, and brain fog. We must learn to unclutter our minds in order to have a flow of ideas and creativity, because creativity is the driver for success in every corner of your life.

The Shower Genius® is a framework you can use over and over. It gives you a template for how to work through issues for yourself, your team, and your family so you can create goals, set expectations, build systems, generate outcomes, and benefit from accountability. It is a full-circle approach to finally alleviate your stress or your teams' difficulties or your family's frustrations. It ties it all up in a big bow to help you create the life (not just the career) of your dreams.

> *Creativity is the driver for success in every corner of your life.*

At my lowest point in 2020, after losing everything for the second time in my life, I was not sure what to do with myself. I found that when I took a shower and was not rushing to get to work, I would have these incredible thoughts and ideas... almost like God was whispering in my ear. It was pretty unbelievable.

I would get excited and finish washing my hair, thinking of all the possibilities.

Then I would get to my desk, ready to make notes and assemble a plan for total world domination,[1] and suddenly, it was all... just gone.

After this happened several times, *I hung a whiteboard in my bathroom!*

Then I could write notes while the ideas were fresh in my mind. This gave me a place to start when I arrived at my desk to

---

[1] A reference to Steven Spielberg's *Anamaniacs* cartoon series in which Pinky always says to his friend, Brain, "Gee, Brain... what are we gonna do tonight?" and Brain always responds, "The same thing we do every night, Pinky... try to take over the world!"

continue brainstorming. This entire book is a result of that process, but I need to give you a little history.

For most of my life, I have struggled with depression, anxiety, and imposter syndrome. I even followed through on my suicidal ideation in 1997 and woke up in the hospital realizing I was still alive. In that moment I did not understand why God saved me, but now, 25 years later, the reason is crystal clear.

I personally suffered with the shame around mental health, staying silent for 23 years about a failed suicide attempt until a colleague in my industry died by suicide. It was my wakeup call. I knew him for more than 20 years. The last time I saw him was at IMEX America 2017 in Las Vegas and we had been trying to get together to have lunch for months after that tradeshow. I was distraught thinking that my story could have given him hope and somehow saved his life. I know it was not my fault, but I still feel like I may have been able to help.

I had stuffed all the trauma and emotions down for decades and had not even processed it for myself. There were so many things around that time in my life I did not remember... but the moment of that split-second decision was, and always has been, crystal clear to me.

I believe God saved me that night so many years ago because I had a purpose in the world that was bigger than me. What I went through was equipping me for that purpose. Now I am thankful for the scars in my journey because I get to use them along with my experiences to help others. In a selfish way, helping others in turn helps me. My coping mechanism has always been work, and I was driven to prove myself to anyone and everyone. It took me the last few years to understand all of this, as well as how putting more value on taking care of myself can in turn change everything about my world.

I wish I had a unique example, but the oxygen mask on the plane, or pouring from an empty cup, are the best ways to explain it so everyone understands.

The Shower Genius® is similar. When we stop to take care of ourselves, we create the wherewithal to take better care of others. When we are exhausted, stressed, and overwhelmed, we can't see the forest for the trees. But when we give ourselves some love and our brains some room, magic happens. The best ideas flow, the creativity takes over, and the path forward becomes easier to discern...

I believe God saved me that night because I had a purpose in the world that was bigger than me.

I created this framework to document it for myself. Then I realized I needed to share it so other people "like me" could benefit. If you identify with any of these descriptors—driven, high achiever, business owner, entrepreneur, executive, planner, ambitious, hard worker, people pleaser—like me, you probably tend to put yourself last on a regular basis.

The event that started me on this journey...

Early in 2018 as I was getting prepped for surgery, thoughts were racing through my head...

Will my team be able to handle everything?

Will that client be upset that I am not at their event?

Is my absence going to hurt my business?

How fast can I get this over with and heal so I can get back to work?

It was all I could do not to jump out of bed saying, "No way can I do this right now!"

But I had been suffering for three decades from what I now know to be endometriosis. I had been to over a dozen doctors, and had endured countless tests on multiple parts of my body over twelve years to figure out why I felt like crap all the time. I finally made it to this point so I could get healthier and feel like a normal human being… *yet my priority was still work.*

Once I came out of surgery, I did not think about work for a while. I was in a lot of pain for a few weeks, so work was the last thing on my mind. After being away just the allotted "two weeks," I started getting antsy, though I still had weeks of healing ahead of me. I was forced to focus on my health.

Once I got better and started to ease back in to work, I realized that my team was already on top of everything, and clients were happy. There was no reason for me to have worried. They were capable, motivated, competent, and I needed to let go of the reins!

After that insightful experience, I started a new plan to take better care of myself.

I had struggled with weight for most of my life, even when I was in great shape. In the months after surgery, I lost about 40 pounds, and one of my employees encouraged me to join the new Orangetheory Fitness® that was opening close to our office. I made every excuse and put it off repeatedly. Then one day, I committed, joined, and showed up for my first class. Let's be real, it almost killed me! But over time, I loved it. I just had to show up and push myself. They told me exactly what to do for 60 minutes. I felt so much stronger and healthier. I bought new clothes that made me feel better, and people were noticing and commenting. I felt more alive, more on top of things, sharper, and all around good! I was still working fulltime and traveling quite a bit, but the shift in self-care and putting my health first was life changing.

Around midnight on March 12, 2020, I landed in Denver after attending a board meeting in Boston with Global DMC Partners. The pandemic was looming, but my team and I were preparing for six European groups to arrive in Denver a couple of days later. Instead, I woke to the state of Colorado being shut down. I went to the grocery store early that morning and was just angry about the whole thing, thinking it would pass and it was no big deal...

I was in denial!

Four days later, I had to lay off my team. It was the worst day of my life.

Ten years of building a thriving business that I started at age 40... but after a few months of the 2020 lockdown, it was clear there was no way the world would go back to normal soon. By July 2020, the writing was on the wall. The following month I closed Realize Colorado.

I thought back to my surgery and how I had believed my business would fail if I was not there every day for two weeks. It turned out that it thrived without me for two months! When the forecast for 2020 had been for double our best year ever... I wondered what might happen if I combined the surgery situation with The Shower Genius® framework of self-care and creativity. I would not only get more ME TIME, but my business and personal life could thrive. I just needed to focus on the parts that I love and my zone of genius.... BINGO!

Boundaries, delegation, and routines are key, but more on that later.

This is the actual whiteboard that I installed in my shower. It helped me to capture my creative thoughts which led to the birth of the framework that led me to write this book.

I am telling you all of this because I personally experienced how self-care breeds creativity, which in turn breeds ideas and solutions, that can in turn change your life in every way. Have you ever wondered why you have the best ideas and revelations when you are in the shower? Or on vacation... (if you actually take one).

A 2018 *Psychology Today* article cited that the shower is the number one place to boost creativity.[2] The article goes on to say that a survey from eight countries found that 72 percent of people reported having creative breakthroughs in the shower. It also stated, interestingly, this was higher than people reporting creative breakthroughs at work.

If we are always working, our brain does not stand a chance at true creativity. "The true sign of intelligence is not knowledge but imagination," said Albert Einstein.

---

[2] https://www.psychologytoday.com/us/blog/the-social-thinker/201803/the-1-place-boost-creativity-hint-you-ll-be-naked#:~:text=Whatever%20the%20breakthrough%2C%20if%20you,creative%20breakthroughs%20in%20the%20shower.

In Reid Hoffman's 2021 book, *Masters of Scale: Surprising Truths from the World's Most Successful Entrepreneurs,* Linda Rottenberg says, "The best ideas don't die in the marketplace or in the laboratory... they die in the shower."

I had a similar experience, but the whiteboard changed the game!

Comments I get from clients:

- ✓ Clients ALWAYS relate to the creativity they have in the shower.
- ✓ They think the whiteboard in the shower is brilliant!
- ✓ They ask about the connection to water, self-care, and creativity.
- ✓ They are surprised by the connection of self-care to the growth of their business.

PHASE ONE: ACKNOWLEDGE & ASSESS

> *"You cannot fix, heal, or express gratitude without acknowledgment."*
>
> —Deana Brown Mitchell

Advice from a River

Immerse yourself in nature
Go with the flow
Go around the obstacles
Stay current
The beauty is in the journey

2 GET FED UP!

> *"Through brokenness I found self-compassion...*
> *It took a while, but I finally got fed up enough*
> *to take steps toward change."*
> —Deana Brown Mitchell

I was that person... always the last one at the office, putting my family on hold to take care of something for a client. I would get excited for a holiday weekend because it meant I could be in the office alone and get "so much work done!"

At one point during my hotel executive days, the 80-hour work weeks were a badge of honor. How did I not realize that this was not OK?

I felt the need to cater to others ahead of myself. I felt the need to prove my worth. I thought their needs were more important than mine, because I could always figure out my stuff later once no one needed my help.

This feeling takes me back to college when I was in Architecture School and working fulltime at a restaurant. Classes all day, bartending/serving/managing all night, then back to Atkinson Hall to work on drawings or models until the wee hours of the morning. There was a couch in the lab and my schoolmates would wake me in the morning for class. I'm not sure why I paid for a place to live!

This continued throughout my career, and many people have said, *"I don't know how you do it."* In retrospect, I did not plan to overwork myself; I just felt driven to accomplish, to achieve, to prove my worth.

When my grandparents would say, "Eat all of your food. There are starving children in Africa," I would clean my plate and then be miserable for hours because I had pushed myself to do something that was not good for my body.

In my hotel days, there were weeks when I actually kept a room in the hotel so I could be there for a client 24/7. I remember a specific week with a client where I worked 120 hours... again pushing myself to do something to please others that was not good for me.

If you are reading this book, I bet you can relate to putting yourself last.

Ready for change?

Are you fed up? What is it that you are doing in good faith that is actually tearing you down? Is it a boss, a client, a colleague, a spouse, a close friend who is pushing you to do things that are not good for you or your health?

Is it YOU pushing you to achieve, accomplish, or prove yourself to someone who does not have your best interests at heart?

Schedule some time alone to **ASSESS** what is wrong with your current situation. Journal or record an audio/video of you ranting about it. This will be the ammunition you need later when you think, *"It's not that bad."* Things will come out that you are not consciously thinking about once you start ranting in a safe space.

What is it that you are doing in good faith that is actually tearing you down?

ACKNOWLEDGE what must change. We must become uncomfortable in some way before we are ready to be the change agent in our lives. Change is hard work.

Work on tackling one thing at a time, because if you try to fix everything at once, you will end up not accomplishing anything.

That will just leave you frustrated and thinking this does not work, just like the *"4 Things to Reduce Stress"* articles I mentioned earlier.

One practice that helped me with change in the past is gratitude. I created a habit for when I was feeling depressed or anxious... I would take deep, slow breaths and think of things in my life that I was truly grateful for. Focusing on the positive is not something I have always done, and I used to hate when people would tell me to *"think of all the things I had going for me."* I did not find that helpful.

It is like addiction, where the addict has to want the change. Someone cannot just tell them they need to change! I was addicted to work and addicted to feeling like the victim.

Once I started practicing gratefulness on my own, it got my mind off the depression and anxiety, and I realized what a great life I had and that my work was going well. It gave me a sense of accomplishment, appreciation, and willingness to keep going. It also brought me to the realization that I was thankful for intangible things like kindness, love, and friendships. Throughout my life I had thrown myself into work so much that I had neglected to spend time with loved ones and friends. Now I wish I could go back and make different choices.

> *It is like addiction, where the addict has to want the change.*

In February 2020, I was six weeks into what would have been my most successful year yet for Realize Colorado. We were onsite for a conference that we had created from scratch for a new client, a year in the making. As we arrived that day, the pandemic was ominous, but we trudged on to make the event successful in every way possible. Ironically this was for the CDC, but nothing to do with the looming Coronavirus.

At the beginning of this event, I received a call that a family member was in ICU needing emergency surgery. I went home a couple of days later, but I should have let my team handle the event and been on a plane immediately. My response was misguided by a need to prove my worth to clients.

For most of us, self-sacrifice is not a heroic attribute. If you are a fireman running into a burning building to save children, that is a different story.

A May 2020 article in *verywellmind*[3] says that twelve characteristics of heroism are bravery, conviction, courage, determination, helpfulness, honesty, inspiration, moral integrity, protective, strength, selflessness, and self-sacrifice. The article also states that empathy and compassion are variables that contribute to heroic behavior.

So, what degree of heroism is okay? How much can we sacrifice without losing ourselves?

> *For most of us, self-sacrifice is not a heroic attribute.*

No wonder first responders, veterans, and superheroes regularly struggle with mental health issues. I agree that all these qualities are incredible, but can they be overdone to our own detriment?

I personally feel that I have these instincts engrained in me, and I mostly use them for good. But when I use them regularly for others to the detriment of myself, then it becomes self-sacrificial.

How far is too far? We must learn to acknowledge this on an individual basis.

We will further explore this topic in Chapter Seven.

---

[3] https://www.verywellmind.com/characteristics-of-heroism-2795943

Questions and comments I get from clients:

- ✓ Clients feel they *must* work as much as they do
- ✓ They do not always see the possibility of change
- ✓ "But I wear all the hats"
- ✓ "Who else is going to do it?"
- ✓ "I would not even know where to start"

Are you ready for change? Are you Fed Up?

What is it that you are doing in good faith that is tearing you down? Is it a boss, a client, a colleague, a spouse, or a close friend who is pushing you to do things that are not good for you or your health?

Is it YOU pushing you to achieve, accomplish, or prove yourself to someone who does not have your best interests at heart? WHAT ARE YOU DOING TO YOURSELF THAT HAS YOU FED UP?

One thing that helped me with change in the past is gratitude. Create a habit for when you are feeling depressed, over-whelmed, or anxious... Take deep, slow breaths and think of things in your life that you are truly grateful for. Focusing on the positive is not always easy but give it a try.

TAKE SOME SLOW DEEP BREATHS...

WHAT ARE YOU GRATEFUL FOR TODAY?

3 WHAT IS MY SANITY LEVEL?

> *"Sanity is our creative thermometer;*
> *when we have lots of it, the ideas freely flow."*
> —Deana Brown Mitchell

Webster's definition of **sanity**:

> *the quality or state of being sane,*
> *soundness, or health of mind*

Do I have a sound mind? How do I know? Could this definition be more vague?

The definition of **insanity** is no better:

> *a severely disordered state of mind*

When I was growing up in the '70s and '80s, anyone who heard the word *insane* would immediately associate it with an asylum, wild eyes, and straightjackets. This is precisely why mental health has such a stigma, hence the silence around the subject.

Since we are talking definitions, **stigma** is:

> *a mark of shame or discredit*

And we wonder why people are scared to talk about mental health...

I struggled for months about what to do with the calling to share my story of suicide. I wanted to help others, but I was petrified of what it would do to my business, my team, and my family.

My first iteration of a plan was to create a give-back side of Realize Colorado (my destination management company from 2010-2020) and create teambuilding/CSR (Corporate Social Responsibility) activities for groups that would somehow increase mental health awareness. In the middle of planning that out, COVID-19 shut everything down.

After I was forced to lay off my team, I proceeded to lose millions in business for the rest of the year. Because *work* was my coping mechanism, and I suddenly had none to speak of, I had nothing to keep my mind busy. I needed something to focus on, so The Realize Foundation, a 501(c)(3) for suicide prevention, was born on March 30, 2020. I was not sure of the plan yet, but dove into research and connected with anyone and everyone in mental health who would talk to me.

The pandemic has shed more light on the subject of mental health, but we still have a long way to go. We have made some strides, for example online therapy and the 9-8-8 national hotline. All of the resources we have access to are needed and helpful to different people in different ways, but they do not address the core problem.

In a July 2021 article by UHC Solutions,[4] I read that one in five U.S. adults has a mental health or substance abuse issue. They said this is a bigger disease burden than even cancer or heart disease. The psychiatric professional shortages have created a huge concern in the healthcare community, citing that the issue is bigger in rural communities. For example, 60 percent of U.S. counties have no practicing psychiatrists. The coverage is also

---

[4] https://www.uhcsolutions.com/2021-mid-year-psychiatrist-shortage-update/

uneven; there are 612 psychiatrists per 100,000 people in New York, but only one per 100,000 in Idaho.

The answer is human connection.

Our mission is to create safe spaces for conversation, community, and personal stories that create connections and let people know they are not alone. There are others in the world struggling with similar, if not the same, adversity we are experiencing.

How This Applies to You

I am sharing all of this with you because it is the journey that led me to writing this book and the framework that I am presenting here. This was my journey to understanding SANITY and how little I had for so many years.

What I have not shared is the shame and guilt I carried which kept me from feeling like I deserved more in life. I felt like I had not done enough to earn the life of my dreams, so I resigned myself to the fact that I needed to settle for mediocre. I kept putting myself last and self-sacrificing in order to keep proving my worth to people who couldn't care less about me.

When it comes to life and personal growth, sanity can take different shapes.

My revelation through this process has been that I do deserve the life I dream of... to spend more time with my family and friends, to achieve the goals I have for success, and to have more ME TIME.

I have learned that when it comes to life and personal growth, sanity can take different shapes.

Sanity is related to all aspects of our lives, from sleep quality to mental capacity. From stress to self-care. From exercise to endless meetings. From activities for kids to date night. From drama at work to judgmental friends. From lack of hope to self-compassion.

Would you like to be able to measure your own sanity?

There are different approaches that you can find, from judicial to psychological data. If you search online for a sanity quiz, beware as they are the definition of insanity!

I created a sensible quiz to help you assess your situation so you can acknowledge what changes you need to make according to the information in Chapter Two.

Use this QR code *(scan it with your phone camera)* to access

THE SHOWER GENIUS® SANITY QUIZ:

It's easy to scan, take the quiz, and get your result within minutes!

TOTAL SCORE_____

Your score will be between 0 and 100. The higher the score, the better your sanity!

Did the quiz help you assess where you are in your sanity journey?

You can take it over and over. You are also welcome to pass it along to others that it can help.

In the case of any life change, we must assess and acknowledge where we stand currently in order to evaluate how to take the first step and make a plan to move forward.

Now you know your starting point!

Simple daily things that help:

- ✓ Drink water, stay hydrated
- ✓ Get outside in nature
- ✓ Human connection/conversation

Questions and comments I get from clients:

- ✓ What do you mean by SANITY?
- ✓ How did you push through the shame to tell your story?
- ✓ I am not sure I can take the first step—it is scary!

Track Sanity Quiz Scores and Progress:

NAME:_____**DATE:**_____**SCORE:**____

Questions with lowest scores (anxiety, overwhelm, etc.):

_____

_____

_____

_____

_____

4 THE VALUE OF RANTING...

> *"I reached a place where change was mandatory, and I did not care what anyone thought."*
> —Deana Brown Mitchell

Now that you have a starting point, let's talk about what's next. Understand that this is the hardest part—to evoke change in your life, to start the ball rolling in the right direction.

I mentioned before that I lost 40 pounds in 2018, and I also lost more than that in 2003. The struggle with weight loss has been a lifelong battle for me. Sometimes I just did not care because I wanted to eat what I wanted to eat, and I dealt with the weight because my urge for pizza was stronger. Both times I lost weight, my urge to do so was stronger than anything I wanted to put in my mouth. I was fed up... I wanted to feel better, I wanted to look better, I wanted more confidence. These things drove me to make the decision to take the first step.

The first week was *hard*, but after sticking to my plan it got better and easier. It was a sense of accomplishment each week that kept me going. I started feeling better, not just in my body, but in my mind... because I did what I needed to do even though it was challenging. It made me feel better about myself and lessened the shame and guilt.

The thing that made my weight loss journey successful was that I removed the obstacles that would defeat my effort. I pre-planned what I was going to eat and had it readily available. I also had a specific plan for myself including rewards when I made it through a week without diverting from the plan.

For instance, if I went to the gym the number of times per week planned, I would get a cheat meal on the weekend. Sometimes the reward would not be food, though. Sometimes it would be a pedicure or a massage. It was always based on self-care.

Out of all the accomplishments in my life, losing weight was the hardest. That is why I like to use it as an example. Change is never easy; that is why we must be fed up to make the decision to take the first step.

Put the Rants to Work

There is a method to this madness... remember the rant exercise in Chapter 2? That is the first step.

Are you sick and tired of being sick and tired? What is it exactly that has you feeling this way? Maybe it is work, maybe it is a personal situation, or maybe it is a person. Put that phone or zoom account to good use and record individual rants about all of the above. Save and label them with the topic and date.

Change is never easy; that is why we must be fed up to make the decision to take the first step.

Set aside some alone time to listen to the most urgent rant you recorded for yourself. Pick out 1, 2, or 3 things that you are most upset about. Take the time to write each one on a piece of paper and brainstorm what steps you can take to change that, whatever it may be.

For example, say I had a rant about "boxes of files that have been sitting in my office for a year that I need to go through and decide what to do with them." I felt like a failure every time I looked at those boxes. It had been on my to do list for over a year. Why could I not just get it done?

My brainstorm list looked like this:

1. Schedule a 2-3 hour window to address the boxes. It could be one night to stay late, an early morning, or possibly a weekend.

2. Make sure it will be an uninterrupted quiet time.

3. Put on a favorite playlist.

4. Have a favorite beverage and snack as a reward when taking a break in the middle.

5. Get it done!

6. Plan a reward for yourself... a movie, a massage, dinner with a friend, date night...

Now, what rant can you address? It may be something with your team, a client, or your family. You can also get them involved. Ask them to do the rant exercise with you so you can all work on the issue as a team.

It could be as easy as "I hate when people leave paper on top of the copier, and someone opens the top and it all falls behind the machine and causes a mess." Or it could be about an issue at home that includes the whole family. For instance, one of your kids could leave all their stuff on the floor when they walk in the front door, and then it is in everyone's way.

I know these examples sound simple, but it is sometimes a lot of simple things that lead to chaos and stress. This is an opportunity to address simple things in a team manner at home and at work to make your days flow easier.

Keep a copy of your sanity quiz. What question had the lowest score? You can use that question as a starting point to create a checklist to tackle. Address items on your list one at a time. Maybe it's anxiety... You can find exercises or breathing techniques to try. Then see what works best for you.

This does not take much time, but you must make it a priority. I found that just taking a walk outside for 15 minutes and breathing in fresh air really helped me when I was stressed or anxious. There is usually a simple solution, but you must be committed to taking the steps and finding what is right for you. It will change your world!

Unclutter

One of the biggest things that helps me, on an ongoing basis, is the act of uncluttering my life. We tend to have clutter on our desk, in our vehicle, in our closet, in the bathroom, in the kitchen, in the garage, and in our mind. Much like those file boxes, we can schedule time for such a decluttering process in all areas of our life.

For me, the satisfaction of cleaning out a space and getting rid of things that I do not use or need is freeing.

It's like having a huge to do list and checking off all the tasks.

We can schedule time for decluttering in all areas of our life.

Organizing and cleaning are similar for me. For many years I felt like I had so much on my plate that I could never get to it all, and I felt bogged down and trapped because of it. I wanted to achieve everything on the list and check it off so I could rest, relax, and be able to decide what I wanted to do with my time.

The act of uncluttering makes me feel like I finished the race and can relax. It makes room in my life and my mind to be creative and decide what is next instead of my to do list dictating my every move.

Weekend Alone

Let's say you have a weekend coming up with no commitments and your family will be out of town. You will be home alone from Friday evening until Sunday night.

The only rule is that you must spend the weekend alone and you must practice self-care.

I want you to stop here and do an exercise with me...

1. Find a comfortable and quiet place.
2. Close your eyes and take 3 deep breaths, slowly in through your nose, and slowly out through your mouth.
3. Visualize yourself getting home from work on Friday afternoon. You are alone with the whole weekend ahead of you.
4. What do you do first? How will you spend the evening?
5. What would your plans be for Saturday?
6. What would your plans be for Sunday?

Get a journal or notebook and write down your thoughts, your plans, and how it would make you feel.

Would you go for a drive, go on a hike, sit by a river, or stay inside?

Would you visit a spa, or go shopping?

You could create your own spa day at home.

Read a book, do a puzzle, watch a movie.

I would love to hear your plans!

Now that you have imagined your perfect weekend of alone time, put it on your calendar and make it a reality. Maybe you cannot have your own house to yourself, but you could rent an Airbnb somewhere you want to go and accomplish the weekend in that way.

Pick a date, confirm you can be off work, make sure your family is taken care of, and then make it happen for YOU! Make room for possibilities, because you deserve it!

These actions will create momentum in your life that will lead to more of the same. If you keep at it, pretty soon it will become a habit. You can't live without ME TIME and self-care.

Questions and comments I get from clients:

- ✓ I would not know what to do with myself!
- ✓ Action Steps.... Think of them as a to do or grocery list.
- ✓ Clean and organize... home, office, car, etc. Declutter.

Ready to Rant?

Are you sick and tired of being sick and tired? What is it exactly that has you feeling this way? Maybe it is work, maybe it is a personal situation, or maybe it is a person. Put that phone or zoom account to work and record individual rants about all of the above. Save and label them with the topic and date.

Set aside some alone time to listen to the most urgent rant you recorded for yourself. Pick out 1, 2, or 3 things that you are most upset about. Take the time to write each one and brainstorm what steps you can take to change that, whatever it may be.

RANT TOPIC ONE:_____

Brainstorm/steps to change:

✓ 1.

✓ 2.

✓ 3.

RANT TOPIC TWO:_____

Brainstorm/steps to change:

✓ 1.

✓ 2.

✓ 3.

RANT TOPIC THREE:_____

Brainstorm/steps to change:

✓ 1.

✓ 2.

✓ 3.

5 DREAM AWAY

> *"Finally took our honeymoon*
> *in our 16th year of marriage."*
> —Deana Brown Mitchell

Now that you have a habit of alone time and self-care, we need to talk about dreaming!

By now you have realized that ME TIME is beneficial in freeing your mind from the stress and clutter. It allows you to see clearly what is possible.

Once you start taking action in the second phase of this framework—Be Your Own Advocate—you will be closer to believing you can have your dream life.

Where to Start

So, what does Dream Away look like? I like to start with your schedule, a practical part of your life that dictates many things.

1. How many days a week would you like to work?

   - How many hours per day?

2. What part of your job or business would you like to concentrate on?

   - What do you enjoy doing?

3. What do you want to delegate?

   - Who on your team could take that over?

- Do you need to hire someone to fill in the gap?

4. What other schedules do you have in your life?

- Community, boards, kids, family...

- How can you simplify those things in order to fit in your dream life?

Next let's talk about vacation, the fun part!

1. How many vacations would you like to take a year?

2. How long should each vacation last?

3. Where do you dream of going/seeing/doing?

4. What is on your bucket list?

5. WHITEBOARD it out, alone or with loved ones. Make it a fun-filled family activity!

Learning to Say NO

After the pandemic took away my business and income, I spent most of my time building my non-profit, The Realize Foundation. But that was not paying the bills and eventually I needed an income from an outside source. I did not mind working, but I needed a schedule that allowed me to keep up the work at the foundation and continue the momentum we had built.

I happened to run into someone who knew me and wanted my help. I was offered a fulltime job but was reluctant to commit. After conversations about my responsibilities, what I needed to accomplish, and my boundaries, we came up with a solution of me working three days a week and I would go in extra if needed to accomplish my responsibilities. This met both of our needs and has continued to allow me to have an income, but in addition, have scheduled time for my other priorities.

This seems like a simple arrangement, but it was a big step for me to create a boundary in my life. Throughout my career I had jumped into every opportunity with both feet and all my time. It felt freeing to say that I was not willing to work fulltime.

Because I said no, the Realize Foundation has continued to create more momentum. It also allowed me to pursue authoring this book, speaking, consulting, and coaching.

Keep dreaming about your own ideal life. Take the easiest, most logical steps first and go through this Assess & Acknowledge process often. It will take time and it will not all happen overnight, but if you keep making time for yourself and keep dreaming, it will happen.

Imagine what is possible. Create your dream life... at home and at work!

In 2010 when I started Realize Colorado, our first logo and tagline looked like this:

It was so clear in my mind that anything you could imagine, you could realize. At the time, I was thinking about events and how we create experiences that change attendees' perspective or thoughts about something in particular. Now, to me it means you can *realize the life you imagine*!

In 2018, I was asked to participate in an anthology called *Journeys to Success, Volume 9*. It was all about how I had used Napoleon Hill's 17 Success Principles of Personal Achievement in my career and businesses.

One of Napoleon Hill's famous quotes from his 1937 book *Think and Grow Rich* is:

*"Whatever your mind can
conceive and believe,
it can achieve."*

If we apply this principle to our situation, there is nothing we cannot accomplish. If you meticulously work your way through this first phase of The Shower Genius® framework—Assess & Acknowledge—it will get you to the first part of the quote. You will be able to conceive or discern what it is you really want. Envision your dream life.

By the end of this book, you will wholeheartedly believe the entire quote can be your reality!

Questions and comments I get from clients:

- ✓ How can I not feel guilty about working less?
- ✓ Won't my clients be upset?
- ✓ You deserve a fulfilled life, and so do your clients! Explain to them what you have learned, and send them this book!
- ✓ If you answer emails at 2:00 am... then that is what becomes expected. Instead, train your clients with good habits instead of bad ones!

What does Dream Away look like? Where do I start?

1. How many days a week would you like to work? And how many hours per day?

2. What part of your job or business would you like to concentrate on? What do you enjoy doing?

3. What do you want to delegate? Who on your team could take that over? Or do you need to hire someone to fill the gap?

4. What other schedules do you have in your life? Community... boards... kids... family? How can you simplify those things in order to fit in your dream life?

Next *let's talk about vacation, the fun part!*

1. How many vacations would you like to take a year?

2. How long should each vacation last?

3. Where do you dream of going/seeing/doing?

4. What is on your bucket list?

5. WHITEBOARD it out, alone or with loved ones. Make it a fun-filled family activity!

Learning to say NO

1. What is it in your life you want to say NO to, but don't think you can?

2. Who would you like to say NO to, and about what?

3. Why do you feel you cannot say NO?

PHASE TWO

BE YOUR OWN BEST ADVOCATE & TAKE ACTION

The Lone Wolf has a strong sense of independence. They enjoy solitude, know themselves well, are not afraid to be different, and the sky is the limit for what they can accomplish.

Deana & Spirit the Wolf

Trust your instincts
Be at home in nature
Keep your den clean
Stand for what you believe
Stay on track
Howl with your friends
Be a leader
Pack life with good memories!

There will never be anyone who can be a better advocate for you... than YOU! If you are allowing your health, sleep, and nutrition to slip, only you are responsible. If you are pushing yourself to work 12, 15, or 18 hours a day, you only have yourself to blame.

In the following chapters we are going to talk about how to stand up for yourself and set boundaries and routines that allow you to be healthy, both mentally and physically.

6 BECOME M.I.A.

> *"Driving my Jeep in the mountains*
> *of Colorado became my safe space."*
> —Deana Brown Mitchell

Sometime in late 2020 I took an online challenge with my friend Francesca Anastasi. She is an incredible human and her instructions changed my perception of myself. On day one, she told us to go in the bathroom, look in the mirror, and say...

"I promise to take care of you mentally and physically every day."

I cried and cried, because I knew I had not taken care of myself in decades, maybe ever. She asked us to post in the Facebook group how this made us feel...

This seems like such a simple exercise, but it changed everything for me because I had never promised myself anything like that, and especially not staring in the mirror! It was profound for me. *I dare you to try it!*

In order to practice taking care of ourselves, we have to become M.I.A. I don't mean disappearing or leading other people to think you are gone without a trace, but rather I want you to create the sense that you are experiencing much needed ME TIME, and no one should bother you.

Missing... Intentionally **A**lone!

One of my favorite ways of doing this before the pandemic was to drive alone in my Jeep. Since my destination management company covered the whole state, and I had lived in twelve different Colorado cities, it was easy to say, "I need to drive from Denver to Telluride tomorrow," which was at least a six-hour trek. Those days gave me freedom to enjoy the beauty of the mountains, maybe with the windows down or the roof off. I could listen to whatever music I wanted and stop for snacks whenever I was hungry.

The other thing it did was give me time to reflect and dream.

How can you take a day or half-day to do something you enjoy? Put it on your calendar and ask someone to cover for you if needed. This is a gift to yourself, so plan something that makes you happy and just do it!

Sometimes, just being home alone to relax or read can accomplish the same thing. Maybe sit in a coffee shop and have a conversation with a stranger. It could be a puzzle, yoga, a movie, an adventure, writing, or journaling... You decide, but no work allowed! This is a time to relax your body and mind.

How can you take a day or half-day to do something you enjoy?

The En Vogue song, "Free your mind and the rest will follow," keeps playing out in my head. Research shows that when you do *free your mind* and eliminate distractions, you create a space for more focus, helping you to push through doubt and create more confidence. This in turn enhances the quality of your life.

When you are unfocused and distracted, it is easy for doubts to creep in. Mental clarity helps you see yourself honestly and non-judgmentally. Instead of worrying about what others think of you, a clear and focused mind will not even entertain those thoughts.

If you can become M.I.A., you can find the ME TIME that recharges you for what is next.

I used to think if I spent 14 to 16 hours a day at my job or business, I was getting so much work done. In reality, my brain was not as productive as it was when I worked for just 6 to 8 hours because I could be more focused for a shorter amount of time.

Right now, as I am writing, I have rules in place to keep me in my most productive state. This can be used in your work environment as well.

1. *Set a timer* for 20 minutes with a goal in mind of what can be produced in that time. You can restart it over and over if you want, but it will give you urgency to accomplish what you set out to do.

2. *Keep a water bottle* by your side at all times. The brain needs water for better efficiency, memory, and focused attention.

3. *Take breaks* when needed to get food and move around to get the blood flowing. At minimum, take a break every two to three hours.

4. *Create a quiet environment* for best focus and productivity.

Think about the times when you are getting ready to go on a trip, a vacation, or taking time away. Do you find that you are in a super-productive mode because you know you will be away for a long period of time?

What if you could be that productive all the time?

The more ME TIME you get, the more focused and productive you can be when you are at work.

For instance, consider packing habits... My husband always packs the day before we leave on a trip. For me, I like to pack in the morning of the trip because I do not want to forget any of the necessities I need to use that last morning. Sometimes I will pack the clothes earlier, then add the necessities that morning, but having it partly done bothers me for some reason.

What if you could be that productive all the time?

My point is that we all have different efficiencies and organizational skills, but as long as we have a system that works for us, that is all that matters.

Have a system for being M.I.A. on a regular basis so your mind stays sharp, and you get the ME TIME you need to keep your sanity!

Questions and comments I get from clients:

- ✓ How can I not be available to my team?
- ✓ What if my family needs me?
- ✓ What if there is an emergency?

Remember the mirror exercise?

You can use one of mine below... or you can make up your own.

What do you need to promise yourself?

Mirror Exercise One:

> "I promise to take care of you
> mentally and physically every day."

Mirror Exercise Two:

> "I am worthy, I am enough,
> and I deserve to put myself FIRST."

Mirror Exercise Three:

> "I will be intentional about
> what I want and go for it."

Your unique mirror exercise:

_____

_____

What is your plan to become M.I.A.??
(Missing... Intentionally Alone)

Pick a date or dates: _____

Pick a place: _____

What are you excited about getting to do during this time?

_____

_____

What outcome are you looking for during this time for yourself?
(relaxing, writing, hobby...)

_____

_____

Other notes:

_____

_____

_____

_____

_____

7 I REFUSE...

> *"When I refused to neglect my health any longer,
> it surprisingly changed more than my body."*
> —Deana Brown Mitchell

Now that we have established how to get more ME TIME and give your mind the space to recharge and think clearly, it is time for the next step...

What do you refuse to do any longer?

Your Job Description

It is time to write your own job description and create your dream life. This is a process that takes time and commitment.

What do you enjoy doing? What are your strengths? What do people count on you to do?

Are you working in your zone of excellence or your zone of genius? *(We will explore this more in Chapter Ten.)*

Why did you get into your career in the first place? What was exciting about it? What was the draw? As children, people likely asked you, "What do you want to be when you grow up?" Whatever your answer was at age eight, it probably changed several times. Maybe you picked a career and stuck with it because it was easier than making a change, but now perhaps it is not what makes you happy.

In my fifties, I think I have finally figured it out!

When I was young, I was interested in doing everything I learned about, and expected perfection of myself every time.

At age four, dance became my world. My dream was to go to New York and become a professional dancer. I was mediocre at best.

I went away to college and decided to major in Architecture. Although I liked it and I learned a ton of practical knowledge, it was not even my zone of excellence. While in school, I worked in the restaurant industry and decided I was pretty good at that. My restaurant career turned into hotels, banquets, and conference services. I excelled in all areas of hospitality, *and* I enjoyed it.

The problem was that I did not know the meaning of ME TIME so I ran myself into the ground working a minimum or 65+ hours a week and usually more. Work was my priority because I felt needed while I was there. It gave me purpose. People depended on me. At that point, *I needed to be needed.*

During the 2008 recession, we moved for my husband's job, and I had some time off to figure out what I wanted to do. That was when I created Realize Planning (Realize Colorado) which was a DMC (Destination Management Company). In the beginning, I worked with corporate clients and handled about 50 weddings in three summers. Then I quit taking wedding business because the corporate business was growing, with work across the state of Colorado. Needless to say, I was working *all* the time. I was also traveling quite a bit and consistently not home. I did everything for everyone and thought that was the only way to succeed.

Let's revisit the story from Chapter One about my surgery in 2018, losing weight, and joining the gym. That was the first time in my life that I was forced to take ME TIME. And I fought it, kicking and screaming all the way! Only once I was released from the hospital did I finally focus on my health and let go of the workaholic in me, at least for a while!

The hardest part about that story was going back to work and figuring out my place. My incredible team had taken care of everything... which meant they did not even need me. I realized how much control I thought I needed prior, and although I was still the boss and responsible for the bottom line, I discovered I did not need to be involved in every event or in every client conversation or decision.

What was a harsh reality, soon became a freeing revelation.

I realized I was in a position to decide what I wanted to be responsible for, when I wanted to work, when I wanted to schedule ME TIME, and how to proceed running my business to accommodate all of the above. I was finally practicing for myself what I had practiced for my team.

> *What was a harsh reality, soon became a freeing revelation.*

When I hired each team member, we discussed what was important to them and set up a job description and schedule based on what they needed to balance their work, family, and personal time. *I had never considered that for myself.* I thought it was my business, and ultimately, I was responsible for everything. That was true, but it is also true that you can set up systems and processes that allow you to be the leader, but not always the executer of all things.

This brings me to the point of this chapter, and this step in the process...

What Do You Refuse to Do Moving Forward?

In my case, I no longer enjoyed some of the duties I had done for many years, in my own business and also in jobs at hotels. I wrote a new job description to focus on client relationships, sales, tradeshows, and serving on boards.

I still had a hand in overseeing all of the marketing, accounting, and event operations, but I did not always even know all the details anymore. In most cases my team did a better job than me because I had been so burnt out from doing the same things for so many years. They had fresh perspectives on things I could no longer see myself.

> *Sometimes we can refuse to do something we just do not enjoy, but at other times we should refuse... because someone else can do it better.*

Sometimes we can refuse to do something we just do not enjoy, but in other situations we *should* refuse... because someone else can do it better. It is not always easy to admit, but it is a way to eliminate something from your plate when you need to learn to delegate.

Do you remember the conversation in Chapter Two about heroism and self-sacrifice? Does it make more sense at this juncture? Whatever you are doing that can be considered self-sacrifice, that is something you need to put in the "I refuse to do" bucket.

So, I will ask again... what will you refuse to keep doing? Remember, you are your own best advocate. You must decide what you are willing to trade for the benefit of your job or business. What is it that you contribute and what is the return?

Once you can put your finger on a list of things that you want on your "I refuse..." list, you can start creating boundaries for yourself.

Here is an exercise that can help provide clarity:

1. Make a list of all the things or duties you do/perform in your job or business.

2. Circle the items you enjoy and look forward to. This is your zone of genius.

3. How can you delegate the rest?

4. Do you need to ask for help? Hire an employee? Outsource to a contractor?

5. Create updated clear job descriptions for each person involved.

6. Create regular reporting systems or touch base regularly to make sure things are running smoothly.

Remember the job I told you about where I decided I was not willing to work more than three days a week so I could concentrate on other projects? That was a huge step in the boundary department for me!

Setting and maintaining boundaries in all areas of your life can help you conserve emotional energy and keep you in a better mental state. Maintaining your assertiveness about the boundaries you have put in place will also help bolster your self-esteem.

You should consider setting boundaries in your personal life as well, at home with family, and with friends.

Another area you can explore is creating boundaries around your own habits. For example, when I cannot sleep, I tend to watch TV or videos on my phone. This is a detrimental habit because it stimulates my brain and makes it impossible for me to get quality sleep. My boundary should be not using my phone while in bed... and I am still working on that one.

What will be your first or next big boundary that you install in your life, work related or personal?

Questions and comments I get from clients:
- ✓ What is my zone of genius?
- ✓ How can I narrow down the list? I enjoy doing it all!
- ✓ How do I delegate or change job descriptions?

✓ How do I hire with flexible terms, or customize?
✓ How do I discover the zone of genius for my employees?

What do you refuse to do moving forward?

Think about the earlier exercise about saying NO...

What came up in that exercise that you want to further explore here?

What would you change about your job description?

What chore at home would you like to get rid of? And how can you make that happen?

8 BE INTENTIONAL

*"Journaling and gratefulness
gave me a new outlook on life."*
—Deana Brown Mitchell

Stop being someone you are not. You do not need to be the person you believe everyone else wants you to be. There is only one of you and you are special with unique talents and skills. Become grounded in yourself, feet in the grass, sun on your face—the way you feel after walking, hiking, skiing, rafting, or accomplishing something you are truly proud of.

Being intentional in every aspect of your life will make change easier.

Now that you have been though the Assess & Acknowledge phase and learned how to become your own advocate, the next step of being intentional is a natural progression. And it is one of the biggest lessons in this book.

Without *intention*, the other steps in this framework do not have the power to change anything. You need the steps thus far in order to become intentional. And the steps that come after this one will be what help you make it all a reality.

*The definition of **intentional***:

> *done on purpose, deliberate*

Once you make decisions around what you want, you must be deliberate in order to make the change.

Routines are one of the best ways you can be intentional. Routines help alleviate anxiety and can promote healthy habits. You can establish routines for self-care, routines for ME TIME, routines for work, for personal time, and on and on. But routines can also become rigid, without flexibility... which means we end up not following them.

You do not need to be the person you believe everyone else wants you to be.

For example, when I owned the destination management company, every day was different. Some days we had departures at 3:00 A.M., other days we had an evening event and worked until 3:00 A.M. Some days were 18 hours straight and others were just working from the office or attending a tradeshow.

My solution was to decide when I needed a routine. Certain things would never happen without intention. Here are a few routines from my list that I established:

1. Quiet time
2. Getting ready in the morning
3. Gratefulness and journaling

I do not necessarily do all of my routines each day, but I practice them as much as I can. If I have a really early morning but can get some downtime before dinner, I will fit in practices I might otherwise only do in the morning. If I needed to be onsite to visit with a client for several 18-hour days, I would make some time when I got home to catch up on some of these items.

Bottom line: *If it is not convenient, you will not do it.*

So you have to figure out how to make it convenient. Also, when you experience these "must do" routines, they need to be fulfilling and meaningful so you will want to repeat the practice over and over. When that magic happens, you will want to make the time in the future, because it's enjoyable!

My suggestion is to look at your schedule weekly. Maybe you have an idea of what you can work on during an early morning or late-night day. When you have an office day, it is likely much easier.

My favorite quiet time is spending 10-15 minutes on my deck in the mornings. It is a peaceful place surrounded by Aspen trees and San Juan Mountain views. I want to spend time there, so I do my best to fit it in each day. There are still days that it does not happen, but I hardly ever miss it two days in a row!

My suggestion is to make a written plan and check in each week at first to see how you are doing. Maybe you need an accountability partner to help you stay on track.

The goal is to be purposeful and intentional with your time, at work and at home. We all have the same number of hours in a week, so if we can learn how to be more aware and spend them intentionally, we can create the life we want to live.

Emergencies Happen

But how can you handle work emergencies? If you know you will need to be away for your own intentional purpose, who can be your backup in case of a work emergency? What constitutes a crisis that would mean someone has to contact you? Make this plan or policy part of your new job description and be intentional about it.

Questions and comments I get from clients:

- ✓ I don't have an emergency backup!
- ✓ How do I make a ME routine?
- ✓ Where do I find an accountability partner who would understand?

How can you be more intentional in your day to day life?

Routines help alleviate anxiety and can promote healthy habits.

Do you have a ME TIME routine currently? If so, what is it? Does it happen daily?

What would you like to do each day deliberately? What time of day would work best?

Some ideas for you to consider:

✓ Quiet time

✓ Exercise (walking, running, yoga, gym, etc.)

✓ Gratefulness and/or journaling

✓ Reading

✓ Self-care (what is your favorite?)

9 CREATIVITY

> *"Oddly, having a degree in design*
> *is not what made me creative.*
> *Being an entrepreneur did that."*
> —Deana Brown Mitchell

Let's talk about daydreaming. If you ask Google about daydreaming, it says that it not only boosts your creativity and problem-solving skills, but it also helps you concentrate and focus on a specific task.

Instead of being considered the escape for losers and slackers, it is now known to be a natural, healthy resting state of the brain. Research shows that daydreaming can be used as a tool to help you through your next big decision or deadline. Daydreaming also lessens stress and anxiety, distancing you from worrisome circumstances.

Again, if you free your mind, you will experience more brain power and productivity.

A March 2021 article from *Forbes*[5] talks about how we were told as children to "get your head out of the clouds and pay attention." Now Erin Westgate, psychology professor and study author, said in a press release, "Daydreaming is part of our cognitive toolkit that is underdeveloped."

---

[5] https://www.forbes.com/sites/alisonescalante/2021/03/23/daydreaming-is-under-attack-now-researchers-say-its-good-for-our-health/?sh=49926d947ee1

When I think of creativity, the first thing that comes to mind is coloring as a kid, drawing as an architecture student, or designing as an event producer.

The definition of **creativity** *that* I *like most is:*

the use of the imagination

Creativity can be so many things... but in this chapter, it is about creating what you imagine for your personal life and career. When you are able to take a step back and give yourself some room to really think about what you want in life... you can get clear about the broad vision, and then hone in on the details one by one.

There are also many processes to create things. Maybe you would like to use a vision board the old-fashioned way, cutting pictures out of magazines. Maybe you want to design it digitally. Or for you, the process could be writing in a journal or on a whiteboard.

If you free your mind, you will experience more brain power and productivity.

As you already know, for me, a shower and mini spa day followed by a whiteboard session is my preferred method of creativity! After the rejuvenating shower and mani-pedi, I am relaxed and ready to put on my creative thinking cap.

Priming

Sometimes I use a priming exercise. If you have never heard of priming, it is a physical exercise that primes your mind and body for optimal brain power. It is great to do this in the morning to come out of a tired, groggy state, or in the afternoon when you need a pick-me-up to become more productive and focused.

This is a fantastic way to relax your mind and get in a creative state.

Priming exercise example:

Sit in a chair with your feet flat on the ground.

As you inhale through your nose, raise your hands straight up in the air (like you were raising a weight-lifting bar).

As you exhale through your nose, bend your arms at the elbow (like you were lowering the weight-lifting bar).

Do this breathing at a rapid pace, three sets of ten inhales/exhales, then rest between sets with your eyes closed.

(You might want to have a tissue handy.)

What Is the Goal of Creativity?

It will depend on your situation and what you are trying to work out, but here are some example goals you've already learned about and can now apply once you're primed and ready:

1. "Dream Away!"
2. Creating boundaries for yourself at work
3. Creating your new job description
4. Creating a routine for your self-care
5. Creating your vacation plan
6. Creating new systems or processes

Plan some time each week to focus on creativity.

Understand when and where you are most creative. For me it is usually early in the morning, in the shower, on my deck, or during a day when I am away from work and doing something I enjoy. What place is inspiring to you? What is your happy place?

Don't think you have to force it. Just relax your mind, enjoy a walk, a run, a workout, sitting in the sun, having a coffee, watching a movie, working on a puzzle, or you can always fall back on taking a shower!

For instance, if you say: "I am going to sit on my porch from 3:00-5:00 P.M. on Sunday afternoon and come up with all my great ideas for the week," it does not necessarily happen that way. But if instead you say: "I am going to enjoy some downtime and sit on my deck and soak up some sun," that is a different story.

You have to create the space and environment, but you cannot force the creative thoughts.

Another way to look at it is to start with a problem that needs to be solved. Say you are stuck on your new job description... you can brainstorm a list of things and then go more in-depth on each idea later to see if it is worth trying. Use your journal or record yourself speaking, or my favorite is still the whiteboard.

You could start with a process you need to create. Maybe it's related to how to distribute information to coworkers or your staff. Assemble the group at a time when everyone is relaxed and not distracted. Talk about the current process and what is wrong with it. Ask for feedback about how it could be done better. Each team member will most likely have a different perspective and different ideas. Once the group comes up with better suggestions and solutions, make it a written policy. Creativity as a group is always better than solo creativity!

> *You have to create the space and environment, but you cannot force the creative thought.*

Maybe the next step is to create and implement a new or different technology to streamline the information. If your team works offsite, then using technology for clocking in and out with a GPS function might make sense in order to have accurate records for payroll or workers' compensation.

Personal growth is another topic you could explore creatively. "How can I do more of what I enjoy at my job or business?" You could investigate a certification, or a time management program, or a development seminar. What tools do you need for efficiency that are not currently available to you and/or your team?

If we look at this from a family perspective, brainstorming at home as a group works, too! It could be meal planning, vacation planning, or just how to get the chores done more effectively.

Let the creative juices flow. Reveal your genius. Be resourceful. Create your vision!

Do not forget the mirror exercise each day!

Questions and comments I *get from clients:*

- ✓ I am not creative.
- ✓ How do I brainstorm?
- ✓ How do I journal?
- ✓ How do I know my growth potential?

What does creativity mean to you?

Remember talking about daydreaming? It boosts creativity and problem-solving skills, and helps you concentrate and focus.

It's kind of like the shower... alone, ME TIME, no distractions. The hot water increases the blood flow to your brain.

What does creativity mean to you?

What creative imagination do you have regarding your career?

What creative imagination do you have about your personal time?

What is your favorite way to be creative, brainstorm, or dream away?

PHASE THREE

GROWTH & FREEDOM

Growth is not just sales and business.
It happens inside of us and changes us.

That change is what gives us freedom to be ourselves
and not fit into anyone's mold.

It gives our mind the freedom to be creative
and express who we are from the inside out.

We all have a purpose in this world.
Don't be scared to shout it from the mountaintops!

Advice from a Mountain

Reach for new heights
There is beauty as far as the eye can see
Climb beyond your limitations
Be uplifting
Savor life's peak experiences
Rise above it all
Rock on!

10 PLANNING & DELEGATION

> *"Planning should be a group activity,*
> *whether with your team or your closest loved ones.*
> *It should not be a secret solution that stays in your head.*
> *It only becomes reality when we share."*
> —Deana Brown Mitchell

Back in Chapter Seven ("I Refuse...") I said we would talk more about your "zone of genius," what it means, and how you can find yours. In 2020, I was gifted a book called *The Big Leap* by Gay Hendricks. One of my biggest personal revelations was about the zones of function.

1. *Zone of Incompetence:* Something you do not enjoy or understand

2. *Zone of Competence:* Something you can do well, but not distinguishing your capabilities

3. *Zone of Excellence:* Something you are tremendously skilled at, and enjoy to an extent

4. *Zone of Genius:* Something that is a natural ability for you, creates success and "flow"

Sometimes the zone of excellence and zone of genius can be confused. Let me explain.

For decades I would have thought that I was working in my zone of genius because I enjoyed what I was doing and seemed to be good at it. From restaurants to banquets, from conference services to my company, it was all hard, but I thought I had found my niche.

After losing everything, needing to start over, and studying this concept, I learned that while I was doing some things in my zone of genius, many of the other things were in my zone of excellence. For me, connecting with and helping people is my true zone of genius. I love to be able to give people solutions to their problems. And if I do not have the answer, I connect them with someone I know who does. This comes naturally to me, and it is fun! I love meeting new people and figuring out ways we can support each other, personally or professionally.

You might have found your zone of genius if:

1. The work you do seems like more fun than work.

2. You look forward to that task, that phone call, or that project.

3. You have a unique understanding or ability regarding your work.

I am curious to know what zone you think you are working in currently, and how you can get to your zone of genius. Look for things that include your passion, skills, and interests.

Once you have a grasp on this concept and practice some creativity around it, you can proceed to *plan* out your next steps:

1. For your work life

2. For your personal life

After this step you will be able to finalize that new job description we talked about in Chapter Seven.

Delegation

What is it that you do in your job or business that you do not enjoy? It is that thing you leave until the end of the day because you just do not want to do it. In fact, maybe you "put it off until tomorrow" several days in a row. It hangs over your head and causes dread.

Who on your team, or in your organization, or as an outside contractor, can take this off your plate? The task might be something so simple as data entry or invoices. Or it could be more complex, requiring a certain set of skills, but there is always someone else who can execute it other than you. And it may even be their zone of genius!

> *Delegation is like daydreaming... it frees your mind to focus on the bigger picture.*

Delegation is like daydreaming... it frees your mind so you have room for bigger and better things! Delegation reduces stress and burnout while at the same time empowers your team to expand their skills and responsibilities. It can also build trust, open communication, and create engagement among your team.

Burnout is real! According to Deloitte[6] burnout affects 77 percent of all employees surveyed. That equates to 3 out of 4 people. And you thought it was just you and you needed to suck it up!

Ready to Plan

Now that you are equipped with knowing your zone of genius, and practicing your creative thoughts and delegation skills, let's look at your new job description which will become the first step of your business/career plan.

If you own your own business, it will be easier for you to make a plan that you yourself can approve. If you have a boss, once

---

[6] https://www2.deloitte.com/us/en/pages/about-deloitte/articles/burnout-survey.html

you have the plan laid out, ask for a meeting to discuss your ideas.

Once, when I was in year three of a new business, I saw a panel discussion about entrepreneurs and how to hire help and create your own job description. I was struggling with this because for three years I had been doing it all, unsure how to hand things off. The suggestion was made, "Make a list of what you like to do then delegate the rest!" It was harder than it sounded but got the ball rolling in the right direction for me at the time.

Maybe your plan will be simple, without much change to your current situation. But do not discount that even little things can change life in your favor. Getting just one task off your plate that takes 30 minutes a day could give you the time you need to walk outside and breathe some fresh air each day.

Even little things can change life in your favor.

If you have a team that reports to you, the plan and job descriptions for each of them is also part of this plan. Hopefully, the team has also been involved in finding their own zone of genius and creative processes. If not, they will need to know about the journey you have been on and why you are looking at change.

Meet with them individually and make sure to understand their needs, both personally and professionally. Discuss their current job description, and what you are thinking about adding or taking away from their plate. How do they feel about that? Possibly offer a course or certification class they have been interested in for their own personal growth.

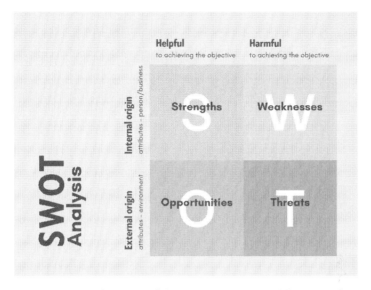

Share a SWOT analysis and let each person fill it out based on their own situation, personal and business. This will help them identify their Strengths, Weaknesses, Opportunities, and Threats. After the zone of genius exercise, this could be repetitive, but can also help to look at things from a different perspective.

You may have team members who have the same job title, but different responsibilities. The more you can customize each person's role to fit their skills, talents, and zone of genius, the better.

I will say it again. Change should be a group effort if you work with a team. Get buy-in at the beginning. Including everyone in the big picture will make everything go much smoother!

Questions and comments I get from clients:

- ✓ What if someone on my team is resistant to change?
- ✓ How can I customize each team member's job description?
- ✓ What is a SWOT analysis for personal growth (instead of a company's growth)?

Let's Talk Planning & Delegation

Have you found your zone of genius?

What is it that you enjoy, is a natural ability for you, and creates success and flow in your life?

How can you plan to do more of that?

What do you need to delegate *(or say no to)* in order to concentrate on your zone of genius?

SWOT Analysis for personal growth:
(Strengths, Weaknesses, Opportunities, Threats)

Make a list of your strengths (zone of genius, skills, etc.):

Identify your weaknesses (things you do not enjoy or are not good at):

Identify any opportunities (new job opportunities, hobbies, purchases, etc.):

Understand your potential threats (competition in the workplace, financial, health):

11 IMPLEMENT

> *"Implementation takes a village.*
> *The more people in the know,*
> *the more success occurs."*
> —Deana Brown Mitchell

Implementation is the last step to making change happen. You have gone through so much to get here! It all started by getting fed up with something that was not working, then doing all the work to get to this final point. Give yourself a pat on the back for making it this far!

The last phase we explored, Planning & Delegation, is crucial to the success of Implementation. So, by this point, your team, family, or anyone else involved in this process should already be intimately involved in the exact steps needed to move forward.

Professional Implementation

On the business side of things, it can be like a conductor leading an orchestra...

Let's use an example from the architecture and construction world. If you were the general contractor in charge of a building project, there is a certain process that you follow. You may have hundreds of workers from multiple companies involved. To implement the construction efficiently, everyone involved must be coordinated by a general contractor. The concrete crew cannot pour the foundation without the utilities in place. The painters cannot show up until the drywall is finished, just like the furniture cannot be delivered before the carpet is laid. And on and on...

If you have a plan to delegate a task to a team member who is not aware of their role, or the process in general, there will be a breakdown in the process, and you will experience failure of the plan.

Processes can make or break a business, a project, or a team. If however, you have the plan, delegation, and implementation down to a science, your organization will run like a well-oiled machine. Still, it only takes one small thing out of place to throw a wrench in the whole operation.

To ensure you experience the well-oiled machine scenario, here are some things to ponder:

1. Is everyone involved in-the-know? Are they on board with their part?

2. Are all processes and job descriptions updated and documented?

3. Do you have the tools needed to execute the plan? (This could be software, supplies, etc.)

4. Are there backup plans in place for each phase of the implementation? Be prepared!

5. What will be considered a successful implementation?

Implementation on the business side could also be something much simpler. Maybe you just need to implement a new process to save time or money in your operation. It could be as easy as developing a new way to share information with your team. When the pandemic forced people to work from home, email replaced the paper inbox on many desks. Changes around that process might have been relatively seamless, but others were not. Many teams struggled to select and implement online video platforms and conquer the associated learning curves.

Organizational implementation can be a huge undertaking. If you consider the planning and delegation in the prior chapter carefully, the implementation phase has the potential of being seamless.

Personal Implementation

You can use the same process in your personal or family life as you do in business. Maybe your family is moving... which is an implementation of sorts. You must create a plan and schedule the timing of many details including the utilities, movers or helpers, the feeding of the family and helpers, the cleaning of the old and new place, and on and on.

I personally have moved 51 times since I got out of high school. Some of those moves were simple while others were very complicated. Some were down the street, and some were across the country. Some involved living in hotels and utilizing storage facilities. But all were carefully planned and implemented to make sure everything was done on schedule and things were left the way they were supposed to be for compliance with whatever rules were in place. Although I would not change any of those moves, I am looking forward to very few moves in the remainder of my life!

We know our own schedule, but those around us may not be in-the-know.

Your implementation could be something much less complicated, like assembling all family schedules on one whiteboard in the kitchen or by the garage door so everyone can be aware of all that is going on. The display could be complete, including carpool assignments and travel schedules.

Sometimes we have our own schedule engrained in our brains, but the people around us may not be in-the-know. That's where there is a potential for an implementation failure! No one wants their child to get left at school because each parent thought the other was in charge of the pickup that day.

If you have a comprehensive plan and everyone is on board, you can avoid the break in communication. Maybe there is a time each week you can hold a family meeting around a fun activity like game night or an outdoor BBQ.

Conclusion

What implementation is next on your list? Is it something you can do individually or something that requires a team's involvement? Is it a family move? A business expansion? A new business venture? Possibly even selling or closing a business, or selling a home?

Whatever it is, I wish you the best and hope you are now prepared in every way to make it a success.

I would love to hear about it!

Questions and comments I get from clients:

- ✓ What if I do not have buy-in from everyone?
- ✓ What if something goes wrong? Or the schedule is off?
- ✓ What if we do not reach the goal?

Ready to Implement?

What is it that you want to implement in these areas
(as a result of your quiz and rants...at home and work):

Daily Routines:

Boundaries:

Vacation:

ME TIME:

M.I.A. time:

12 GROWTH & RESULTS

> *"Growth is a continuous process;*
> *it is not a one and done,*
> *in ourselves or in business."*
> –Deana Brown Mitchell

It's GROW time! You have done the arduous work of planning and implementing and now it is time for growth. No matter what part of your life we are talking about, growth is essential for change.

*The definition of **growth** is:*

> *a stage of increasing, developing, or maturing*

Growth can happen in all areas of your life. When you are born, you do not really have a choice about growth or change, and you are left to figure out along the way how to cope with what happens to you. You learn how to walk and talk, and not to touch a hot stove.

As you get older, you gain a bit more control over the change in your life. Sometimes you make bad decisions or good decisions, and you learn and grow from all of them.

Once you have a spouse or children, the growth shifts to a new level because it involves other people. Your decisions have a ripple effect on those who are close to you... and that comes with more responsibility.

If we are talking about business, your decisions have more influence throughout your organization. They may also affect clients, vendors, and contractors.

Since you are on a mission for change in both your personal and professional life, it is important to measure your results along the way. You must understand the fruits of your labor and consider how they align with the expected outcome.

Your decisions affect those close to you... and that comes with more responsibility.

Think back on the journey it took to get here. Where were you when you started in the "Fed Up" stage at the beginning? Take some time to reflect on the work you put in from there to here. It is a process that takes commitment and hard work. You did it! Now watch and learn from the growth that happens because of the time you put in.

Continue to closely monitor your situation. Do you need to adjust something in your plan or implementation in order to get or keep the expected outcome?

Maybe the results have exceeded your expectations. If so, make sure to document these results as a benchmark so you can analyze what worked and what did not work. Get feedback from the team involved, because maybe they have a different perspective than you or a different view of how it all came together.

The more you can study and document your results, the more productive you can be moving forward, and the more you can learn about what to do next. It is also important to get customer or client feedback when relevant.

It's not only for business though. You also want to look at results on the personal side of things. It could be the result of a family vacation, or a new routine, or your ever-developing ME TIME plan.

The plan for me was about losing weight. I lost over 40 pounds... *twice*. But both times, I gained it all back. Of course I have been blaming the most recent time on the pandemic and the fact that my gym was closed and now I live in a different place without that gym.

> *We usually have more control over our situations than we like to admit.*

But am I right in blaming those things? While they were contributing factors... it is no one's fault but my own. For over a year I was not fed up enough to do the hard work to change anything.

We usually have more control over our situations than we like to admit.

No matter how you look at it, you have control over the growth and results in your life. If you are willing to put in the work and be your own best advocate, you can do anything you put your mind to.

Get Grounded

The exercise of getting grounded always helps with discernment around your place in the world and the thoughts in your own head. It will help you stay calm and quiet the anxiety or negativity.

There are several ways to do this including breathing deeply, putting your feet in the grass, soaking your hands in water, sitting in the sun with your eyes closed, listening to music, hanging out with a pet, or just making a statement (saying it out loud) about an obvious fact in the present.

I remember when I first learned to downhill ski. Although I was petrified at the beginning, it was exhilarating. To have the cold wind on my face and conquer the mountain (big or small) made me feel alive and that I could accomplish anything. Whitewater rafting gave me the same energy. I know—I am an adrenaline junkie and not everyone thinks those things are fun... but what is it for you that makes you feel alive?

We can all achieve what our mind can conceive. Through measuring growth and results, you can prove it to yourself and others. So, get an empty journal or notebook and document what you have achieved through this process. Then make a list of what is next!

Questions and comments I get from clients:

- ✓ What if I did not get the anticipated results?
- ✓ What if I exceeded the expected result?
- ✓ What is the best way to analyze and measure growth?

Let's Analyze Your Results:

Growth is a continuous process. So let's document your progress and analyze what's next! Start with the Quiz Tracking worksheet to look back and see where you started and how far you have come in each question category.

Where did you see the biggest change through this process?

What Routines did you implement, and how have they affected you?

What Boundaries did you implement, and how has that changed your life?

If you did not get the results you intended, why do you think that is?

What would you like to do next? What change do you want to rant about?

13 RINSE & REPEAT

> *"The Shower Genius® Framework is meant to use over and over. When you feel stuck in life, it is there for you. Whether it is a new business challenge or a personal obstacle, this process can help."* —Deana Brown Mitchell

What is the next thing you want to change or accomplish? To be effective, you can only tackle one obstacle at a time. It may be a new morning routine. Once you have it mastered for 30 days, you could move on to hitting a huge sales goal at work which might take 12 months.

Be careful not to bite off more than you can chew at one time!

Commit to the small step of a single change, then once you have it conquered, use the framework again for the next thing on your list.

Keeping a notebook or journal for your running list of changes and accomplishments for which you are striving will make this process easier. Document your steps and changes. Revisit your notes often, reminding yourself what is next as well as all you have conquered!

Be careful about starting multiple goals at the same time, as it is all too easy to wind up in a situation where you do not achieve any of them. That is what discourages us from trying new things again, or from being successful in achieving the one or two changes we really want in life.

Sanity 2.0

Let's revisit sanity. At this stage, it is a great time to go back and take the Sanity Quiz again and see what has changed. This is another way to analyze and measure your results. See how far you have come now that you have gotten through the entire process!

For example, the first problem you tackled was designing that weekend alone. How difficult was it to make that happen? How rewarding was it to actually experience the ME TIME? What creativity came from that experience and what ripple effect did it have in your life? What did it change in your mindset?

Time alone for anyone is crucial, even if it is only in the shower. We all need time to gather our thoughts, relax, recharge, and practice self-compassion. Self-compassion is the act of kindness to ourselves. It is the acknowledgment of our own thoughts, feelings, and pain. How can we be more patient and accepting of ourselves in every way?

There is only one YOU. The skills, talents, insights, and personality you possess is only yours. You matter, you are enough, and you are worthy of your dreams. You deserve everything that you envision for yourself!

If you are anything like me, you have to give yourself permission to believe that last paragraph. You have to give yourself permission to be YOU and not just the person you believe others think you should be. You are unique and made to be just who you are, inside and out. The world needs the skills and talents of the *true you.*

> *You matter.*
> *You are enough.*
> *You are worthy*
> *of your dreams.*

At age 50, I finally realized the truth inside this concept. I spent five decades trying to prove that I was someone I thought others wanted me to be, both personally and professionally.

There will always be humans who do not agree with you, or who think differently than you. But each of us has a special place in the world and we do not all need to agree on everything.

Stand up as your true self, become your own advocate, dream away, and reach for the stars!

My hope is that this framework has helped you meet your true self so that you might discern what you really want in your life.

What are you fed up with now? You can just rinse and repeat the process, reading and re-reading this book, so you can keep checking things off the list!

Questions and comments I get from clients:

- ✓ How do I be myself in a professional setting and still maintain the respect of my team?
- ✓ How do I find the right grounding exercises for me?
- ✓ How do I decide what is next?

Retake the Sanity Quiz:

Track Sanity Quiz Scores and Progress:

NAME:_____**DATE:**_____**SCORE:**___

Questions with lowest scores (anxiety, overwhelm, etc.):

_____

_____

_____

NAME:_____**DATE:**_____**SCORE:**___

Questions with lowest scores (anxiety, overwhelm, etc.):

_____

_____

_____

NAME:_____**DATE:**_____**SCORE:**___

Questions with lowest scores (anxiety, overwhelm, etc.):

_____

_____

_____

14 MY HOPE FOR YOU

> *"My hope for you is that you learn to put yourself first and realize the life you imagine. It IS possible!"*
> —Deana Brown Mitchell

Since this is Chapter Fourteen of the book, I would like to share a personal story about the number 14 with you...

I have lived in Colorado since 1999 except for a few years, and I have lived all over the state. We have 58 mountains that are over 14,000 feet in altitude. The locals affectionately call them "14-ers."

The first 14-er that I climbed was Handies Peak (14,058'), in 2001 with three friends. I wore shorts and a fleece, and the only gloves I had were my neoprene rafting gloves. Needless to say, I was a little underprepared for implementation!

It was not long after September 11, 2001, and while I felt a sense of accomplishment standing on that peak with incredible views, there was also a sadness about our world that I could not shake.

Years later, I also climbed Mt. Elbert (14,438') which is Colorado's tallest peak, and Mt. Sherman (14,043').

Mt. Elbert Summit, tallest peak in Colorado.

I share this with you because we all have mountains or obstacles in our lives that we have climbed or conquered. Telling my story of suicide publicly was harder than any physical mountain I have ever climbed.

Pre-COVID, my "mountain" was creating the plan to sell my business and retire with my husband, but that plan came crashing down in 2020. Although I lost everything I owned, it was a blessing in disguise.

Starting over for the second time at age 50, I found my true purpose in this world. Without the failures and the lessons, along with what I learned about self-care and sanity, this book would never have come into existence.

There are mountains out there for all of us, and you will want to climb or conquer them. What will be your first or next mountain? Choose something you want to accomplish for yourself, your health, or your personal development.

My hope is that this process will help just one other person get the life of their dreams... but my wish is that it will help thousands, because everyone deserves to reach their potential and have a fulfilled life!

Through my non-profit, The Realize Foundation, I now have seen the ripple effect it has already made in the world of mental health and suicide prevention. I know that this book and framework, along with the aligned online course, will have the same effect for many more lives.

I am thankful for losing my business, because I finally got my life, my passion, and my purpose in its place.

I wish the same for you,
Deana

Questions and comments I get from clients:

- ✓ How do I take the Sanity Quiz?
- ✓ How do I get my results?
- ✓ How can I connect with Deana?

Offerings

Although you have all the tools you need in these pages to make radical changes in your life, there are other resources available to you.

If you need accountability, community, or personal interaction to make more progress in a shorter amount of time, check out the course.

The course allows you to go at your own pace, but also be supported by me and our community through the process.

Schedule a call with me to discuss:

deanabrownmitchell.com/connect

Learn more about The Shower Genius COURSE:

deanabrownmitchell.com/the-shower-genius

Here is what is included:

* 6-month access to videos and worksheets

* Weekly Zoom calls, and live Q&A with Deana

* Two 1-on-1 calls with me, scheduled when you need them

Check out the course link for bonuses, details and more!

About the Author

DEANA BROWN MITCHELL is an entrepreneur, mental health advocate, speaker, coach, and best-selling author. She started her entrepreneurial journey at the age of 14. She holds a Bachelor of Architecture degree from Louisiana State University and has enjoyed a three-decade career in the hospitality and event industries.

As the President of Genius & Sanity, her mission is to share experiences of how putting yourself first changes everything. The focus is to find the balance in career success and whole self-health.

In 2020, Deana founded the Realize Foundation which is dedicated to reducing the statistics of suicide by fostering human connections through conversation, community, and personal story.

Learn more at:
deanabrownmitchell.com

Printed in Great Britain
by Amazon

86901546R00062